Why Be Jewish?

Also by David J. Wolpe

The Healer of Shattered Hearts:
A Jewish View of God

In Speech and In Silence:
The Jewish Quest for God

Teaching Your Children About God:
A Modern Jewish Approach

Why Be Jewish?

DAVID J. WOLPE

HENRY HOLT AND COMPANY ✦ NEW YORK

Henry Holt and Company, Inc.
Publishers since 1866
115 West 18th Street
New York, New York 10011

Henry Holt® is a registered trademark of
Henry Holt and Company, Inc.

Library of Congress Cataloging-in-Publication Data
Wolpe, David J.
Why be Jewish? / David J. Wolpe.
p.   cm.
Includes bibliographical references and index.
1. Judaism—Essence, genius, nature.   2. Jewish way of life.
I. Title.
BM565.W63   1995   94-48199
296.7—dc20   CIP

ISBN 0-8050-3928-7
ISBN 0-8050-3927-9 (An Owl Book: pbk.)

Henry Holt books are available for special promotions and
premiums. For details contact: Director, Special Markets.

First Edition—1995

Designed by Victoria Hartman

Printed in the United States of America
All first editions are printed on acid-free paper. ∞

10   9   8   7   6   5   4   3   2   1

10   9   8   7   6   5   4   3   2   1

(pbk.)

For Eileen

CONTENTS

PREFACE

For many Jews, religion seems an antique and unyielding system that no longer fits our lives. Having learned little about Judaism since childhood, we remember our religious education as a jumble of curious legends and ideas. We feel ourselves to be sensitive, perhaps even spiritual people, but organized religion is associated with boredom at best, narrowness at worst.

Yet as I travel around the country, speaking and meeting with various groups, I encounter thousands of people who are exploring religion, spirituality, and Judaism. Some are asking deeper questions of life after having made a place in their careers or community. Some are now planning a family and wondering what to teach to their children. Some are just beginning to forge their own paths in the world and want to start out with a clear, persuasive explanation of where they come from and what their legacy means.

Still others, born into another faith, are contemplating marriage to a Jew and seek to understand what this tradition and people are all about.

Such a list hardly exhausts the kinds of people who are wondering, Why be Jewish? If this question has stirred your soul, or perhaps simply roused your curiosity, this book is for you. *Why Be Jewish?* is not a full-fledged introduction to Judaism but a personal portrait of faith for those who are searching: an attempt to show in quick, large strokes what this remarkable faith is really about and how it can transform your life.

In each of its three chapters, the book explores an answer to the question, Why be Jewish?: to grow in soul, to join a people, and to seek God. The text is intentionally short and to the point. It is not intended to explain all of Judaism but rather to guide you to its heart.

For thousands of years people have found Judaism a rich, artistic, and holy path of living. There is an enormous effort in our time to seek out ways to lengthen life. Here is a way to deepen it.

ACKNOWLEDGMENTS

This book began with a conference in Oakland, California, at which I was asked to address the question "Why Be Jewish?" The response to that talk, which brought letters and visits from attendees, convinced me that this most fundamental question was often neglected. While many explained what Judaism was about, there was less discussion of why it was so vital to people's lives today.

I was fortunate to be able to write this book while teaching at the University of Judaism in Los Angeles. In the decade I have spent there as a student and a teacher I have been constantly enriched by its atmosphere and its mission. *Why Be Jewish?* also profited from the help of a number of friends and colleagues: Robert Wexler, Daniel Gordis, and Mimi Sells, all of the University of Judaism; as well as Joseph Telushkin, Lynn Nesbit, and my editor Marian Wood, whose knowledge of books is second only to her insight into her authors. Finally, my greatest debt is to Eileen, who supplies love, wisdom, and patience in equal, unending measures.

Why Be Jewish?

We are God's stake in human history.
Abraham Joshua Heschel

✦ ✦ ✦

All beginnings require that
you unlock new doors.
Rabbi Nachman of Bratslav

· 1 ·

TO GROW IN SOUL

The human soul is the candle of God.
Proverbs 20:27

The Secret and the Mystery

Inside each of us is a secret searching for a mystery. The secret we carry is uniquely our own. We can share it with others, but we never lose it, like the candle whose light kindles a new flame without being itself diminished. We can hide our secret, hoard it, damp it down until it is almost extinguished, but we cannot fully destroy it.

The mystery is what to do with our secret. When we are young, the secret seems something both wonderful and trivial; we play at it, expand it, and dream that it will one day matter. But it is only as we grow older that we are captured by the force of the mystery: for the secret is our soul, and the mystery is how to tend it and help it grow.

The world blares at us. Each morning as we arise we hear the screech of the headlines, demanding our attention. This is what you must hear, think, give yourself to *right now*. Tomorrow the issue will be different, but it is never less than urgent, never less than loud. The melody of the self, a strain so thin and delicate, has little chance to be heard. Listening takes time and silence, and in the frantic noise we lose attunement.

One solution is to close out the world. Retreat, ignore the clatter of the street. But isolation is at best a temporary solution. The world is the stage of all drama. To be healthy, a soul has to care about other things and other souls beside itself and its source. If all we attend to is our own cultivation, we are listening not to the call of the soul but the tyranny of the ego.

To believe in our secret and tend it is a beginning. The spark of soul inside each of us is unique. Out of the billions who live, who have lived, no one has shared exactly our secret; no one will ever be as close to it or understand it as we do. To lose that in the surface turmoil of everyday life is a tragedy.

A soul is both a hearty and a fragile thing. So long as there is life in us it persists, yet it is easily chilled or silenced. The mystery is to find a way to live in a frantic and fast-paced world that does not do violence to our conscience, that does not stunt our souls.

✦ ✦ ✦

Not long ago I sat on a porch in Jerusalem. It was early, and the sun had not yet risen. The city was still. The streetlights dotting the dark began to give way to the glow of the sun sprinkling pink on the Jerusalem stone with which the city is built. The moment was exquisitely quiet; I felt as though the sun, the city, and I were secret companions.

But the silence did not last. As the light stretched through the streets, striking windows and rooftops and doors, it began to coax people from their homes. Cars pulled onto the streets, and the sounds of the city, harsh and insistent, made the rose-glow silence of an hour before seem like a dream.

Yet the silence and the stones and the soft gleam of the sun were real, and indeed they still lay beneath the bustle of the city. I had seen them; I had been there. They left a gentle mark on my memory. The question for me that day—and in a different form every day—is whether I can retain that moment of magic as I go about my work, when the sun is bright, the stones are bleached from the heat of day, and all the harsh sounds of the city surround me.

That early-morning moment represents for me the time when I can hear the notes of my soul and feel its connection to its Source. But the world is not all dawns and evenings, and it will not keep quiet so that we can hear the rustling inside of us. The world will present challenges to distract or dissuade us from trusting that moment: the busyness of the day, the triviality and sensationalism that competes for our attention, the cynicism of others, and the sheer difficulty of moving attentively through life. In the clamor of the day, the secret seems a fantastic invention of the night.

What helps me to keep the Jerusalem dawn as the day moves on—indeed what brings me to that city in the first place—is Judaism. Judaism is a life system that encourages spiritual awareness and moral passion. It forbids us to disregard the sometimes discordant music of the world but also teaches how to cultivate the song of the individual soul. It involves both the ardent thirst for the justice of the prophet and the quiet, early-morning meditation of the mystic. Judaism teaches souls to grow by paying attention to more than themselves alone.

Judaism is the mystery that the secret searches for.

The Start of the Journey

The Bible portrays the origin of Judaism in God's call to Abraham. Abraham is told to leave his childhood home, told to go "to the land that I will show you" (Gen. 12:1). The life he has known is overthrown in that instant. Abraham has been fated to follow something grander and deeper.

God does not tell Abraham his destination, because the goal cannot make sense to someone who has not yet experienced the journey. Arrival is not the essence. The lesson that Abraham will pass on to his descendants is that the key to the journey is the journey.

The command to Abraham "*Lech L'chah*" (Go forth) is literally "Go, you." The Hebrew can also be read as "Go to you," that is, journey inside yourself. Moving through this world is always an expedition into the "you"—into one's own soul. Abraham must be willing to leave the community that will not accept his changed spirit. But even more important, he must be willing to break with what has been inside of him until this moment.

In Abraham's time as in our own, most are content to skate along the surface of their lives. God's call in Judaism is a challenge to go deeper, which means a challenge to wrestle with difficulty. Abraham must stop looking back on the life that has been provided for him; he must change his focus and look forward to the life he is fashioning for those who will come after. He is no longer just an inheritor but a creator, not only a descendant but an ancestor, no longer a passive recipient of the ideals of others but an idol smasher. The moment that Abraham responded to God's call by saying, "I am here," his soul burst out of the cage of convention and began its journey.

This is the model and the challenge for one who undertakes a truly Jewish journey. Quiet and complacency tempt one all along the way. But the call to depth is always there. "Go forth" has no ending—not in the world and not in the terrain of the individual soul.

Jews are called the children of Sarah and Abraham. That is not a statement of biology; it is a statement of destiny. But none can claim a destiny who will not journey.

Judaism's Central Teaching

Why is Abraham—or any human being—worthy of such a challenge?

Judaism's most important single teaching is that each human being is created in the image of God.

Historically this teaching was revolutionary. Until Judaism brought this idea to the world, different values were placed on the lives of different classes of people. Even into the Middle Ages, the *wergeld* (man-price) for a subject who was killed depended upon the victim's status. A serf was worth less than a land-owner, and a murderer was penalized accordingly.

But the Bible* insists that the intrinsic value of each individual life is the same. God's image does not grow or diminish with income or social status. All of humanity is bound together. Judaism introduced the idea that all human beings are family, all children of the same eternal parent. Each soul bears a spark of the Divine.

What part of us reflects that Divine image? Is it in our reason, our speech, our eyes or smile? By image do we mean something physical or something spiritual?

The Divine image is the part of ourselves we *cannot* point to. It is not in your eyes or your reason or your sense of humor. It is what makes each of us unique, unmistakably and ineffably ourselves—unlike any other human being who has ever lived or who will ever live. It is what makes us equal, for we are all in God's image but different, for we are all unique reflections of that image.

The mystics speak of the spark of God that enters into each individual. As God is infinite, so the sparks are infinite. Each person carries his or her own spark. Therefore the central challenge in each life has noth-

---

*The Hebrew Bible, called by some the Old Testament. Another name for the Bible is the Torah, a word sometimes used to refer particularly to the first five books of the Bible and sometimes expanded to mean the whole corpus of sacred Jewish teachings.

ing to do with appearance or intellect or energy or connections or wealth. The source of self-esteem and worth is not ultimately in talent or drive. The Divine spark is the decisive part of our essential nature. That spark can be fulfilled or betrayed, made monstrous or glorious.

To carry inside of us something of the Divine, to glow with embers of an eternal flame, seems too much for us to believe or to bear. So we often belittle it or toss it aside. We call it hubris to insist that we are important. We are no more than animals or collections of chemicals.

Samuel Johnson once wrote that behaving like a beast frees one from the pain of being a man. Similarly, to believe that we are nothing but a complex of chemicals frees us from the burden of being souls, of being partners with God in the betterment of the world. It would be easier to believe that we are accidental and our deeds inconsequential. Indifference takes no energy. But living as though one does not matter is to forsake one's soul.

Understanding how important we are is imperative, but it carries its own dangers. For at times we suffer from the opposite of indifference, and our arrogance carries us away. We imagine ourselves masters of all that exists and forget our own fragility and dependence.

But that arrogance is usually a disregard for the real

sources of our stature and worth. In the biblical Book of Samuel, Saul is stripped of the Kingship of Israel. The reader might at first assume that it is because Saul has grown too arrogant. But Samuel, who has seen more deeply, sums up the true nature of Saul's sin: "Are you small in your own eyes? You are the King of Israel; and God has sent you on a journey" (I Sam. 15:7).

Each of us, bearing God's image, shares the predicament of Saul. It is a sin to be small in our own eyes, even if we cloak that smallness in a mantle of conceit. We are each sent on a journey. To make progress takes more than a stiff spine; it takes a searching soul.

Judaism teaches us how to balance. It reins in our arrogance; we are, after all, nothing beside the vastness of the world and the incomprehensible nature of the world's Creator. Judaism teaches us how to feel the awe, the stupefied silence that appropriately greets a glimpse of the power of the unfathomable.

But at the same time Judaism will not permit our posture to be simply one of kneeling. In the Book of Ezekiel, when God first approaches the overwhelmed prophet, God says, "Stand upon your feet, that I may speak to you" (Ezek. 2:1). Human beings bear God's image; we bow down in devotion, but we stand up in mission. To carry God's word and will into this world is not a trivial task and cannot be accomplished by remaining on our knees. Those who jeer at humanity betray the most important thing about us: the sacredness of our obligation to ourselves, to each other, and to God. Though we are not always noble, our purpose is, and only by a combination of ego and effacement can we fulfill the proclamation of the prophet: "None shall hurt nor destroy in all my holy mountain. And the earth shall be filled with the knowledge of God, as the waters cover the sea" (Isa. 11:9).

What Is Spirituality?

What does it mean to be a spiritual person? Sometimes the idea is trivialized, and a spiritual person is thought of as one with a faraway look and a cryptic smile. But true spirituality is both more mundane and more mysterious.

Being spiritual cannot simply mean that we feel good or even exalted. It means more than enjoyment or celebration. Spirituality is a stirring in the depths. Spirit originates beneath the surface, though the surface experiences of life are often what enable us to explore more deeply.

One of the lessons of spirituality that Judaism teaches is that spirituality is not a solitary affair. True spirituality means a relationship with other human beings and with God. Spirituality is expressed in the bridges we forge with others from the center of ourselves. We come to a spiritual relationship by the deep and constant exploration of our own souls.

That exploration is not always smooth or easy. To be spiritual requires breakage. The Rabbis of the Talmud* teach that, unlike human beings, God loves broken vessels: those who are open enough, humble enough, to allow themselves to be cracked, hurt, and healed. If we are always shoring up our defenses inside, terrified of being touched, shrinking back, interpreting gestures of love as assaults, there is no place for another to enter. Openness is not only vital to human connection, it governs our relationship with the Divine as well. To be a spiritual person means to seek out others, including God, and to permit them to seek back. It means to pry oneself open, while knowing that vulnerability is not a constant condition; there will still be other times of hiding and even escape.

Spirituality reaches toward attunement with self and toward deep relationship with others and with God. Being spiritual means treasuring your secret but not locking it away, seeking always to grow in soul,

---

*The Talmud is the most important book in Judaism after the Bible. It is a massive work, compiled over approximately seven hundred years, from 100 B.C.E. to 600 C.E., by Rabbis, who are the principal interpreters of the Jewish tradition.

and acting in a way that dignifies the specialness of being human.

Spirituality does not rest content with what our senses perceive. The invisible part of the world is alive to those who seek to see with an inner eye. The invisible reality permeates the material world; trying to separate the two is impossible. In the image of the poet Keats, it is like trying to unravel a rainbow.

The oldest and best-known homage to that invisible reality is Judaism's battle against idolatry. Judaism's constant struggle with idolatry reminds us how powerful are the images that we can see; so powerful that our ancestors often prayed to the forces of nature embodied in statues and stone. We are not free even today of the worship of the visible, the adoration of the material, the impulse to treat the products of our own hands as of ultimate importance. We see limited things, material things, as all significant. Spirituality is a constant striving to keep in mind the truth that the intangible is ultimate, that the moral world spins on the axis of what we cannot see.

Judaism is as ancient a system as exists for training our inner eye to perceive the intangible wonder of the world. Judaism makes the term *spirituality* really mean something, instructing us to develop our relationships and sharpen our senses and teaching us actions that deepen our souls.

Inside each soul there are chambers, and chambers

within chambers. Most of us open the door to a few compartments of our soul and leave the rest undisturbed. Judaism impels us to keep looking and, in the process, to discover that as we open these chambers to ourselves, we are more open to God as well.

Spirituality is also concerned with shaping our actions and, through them, touching the tender part of our souls. As action and passion interact, we are slowly changed, moving closer and closer to the ideal of a true sage enunciated in the Talmud—one whose inside and outside match. Spirituality means transforming oneself; a religious tradition is a system that teaches how and in what direction we should change.

✦   ✦   ✦

A medieval Rabbi once explained prayer with a wonderful parable. When we pray, he said, we think we are changing God. Think of a man in a rowboat who is pulling himself to shore. To someone who did not know what was going on, it might appear that he was really pulling the shore closer to himself. Similarly, when we pray, it may appear that we are trying to pull God closer to us. But we are really pulling ourselves closer to God.

Judaism throws us the rope.

Science and Spirit

To believe in the potential goodness of human beings, to see them in God's image, to act with goodness—all of this reinforces Judaism's idea that we must seek to raise ourselves above the animal, appetite-driven part of ourselves and into the realm of spirit. If human beings are more than physical, if we are creatures of spirit as well, then cultivating spirit becomes our great task. In our scientific age, when we have learned so much about the nature of the world, we begin to believe that nothing that cannot be dissected or measured or seen can exist. Judaism recalls us to our deeper dignity; beyond science is sanctity. We cannot change the world and leave our souls untouched.

Science has revolutionized our lives, often dramatically for the better. It has taught us unprecedented and fascinating things. Yet it has costs. Sometimes intellectual achievements divert us from the center of our own beings. Science involves looking outward. The scientist must be separate from the object studied in order to gain intellectual mastery over it. Sanctity asks us to look within as well as without and to judge not by a scale of mastery but by a scale of reverence.

To make a commitment to the reality of the unseen is not to deride science. The Rabbis state that "the seal of God is truth" and an honest faith must be consistent with what is true. To close our minds to evidence is to admit the weakness and narrowness of faith. True faith today, as ever, is supple and strong.

For all its power, science cannot be the meaning of our lives or tell us why to get up in the morning. Supreme at *how* questions, science does not answer *why*. That is the function of faith.

The human race has always battled with its own creativity. Technological inventions have been blessings, but they have also created mechanisms of destruction and annihilation. Without a belief in something deeper than the material workings of the world, humanity's fragile grip on goodness easily slips. All the blessings of our age will be vain if we permit science to strip us of soul. Human skill creates marvels; still, we cannot let the products of our hands divert us from the prompting of our hearts.

The Truth About Human Nature

Being in God's image is an ambiguous legacy. For although God may overflow with goodness, we imperfect reflections of God do not. We are struggling creations who seek to be better. We often fail. Falling into evil is so easy.

Judaism is powerfully focused upon goodness because to be good takes work. A simple exhortation to be good is not enough; both our history and the world as we find it today remind us that human beings have enormous appetites for cruelty and destructiveness.

Along with cruelty, however, we have strong impulses to goodness. Disentangling the good and the bad within us is perhaps impossible. In an instructive fable, the Rabbis of the Talmud imagine that one day the evil impulse in human beings was captured and bound. Suddenly, no one had children, built houses, or took initiative, for our drives are complex and interrelated. Ambition, sexuality, even envy—all of them can be creative or calamitous.

Judaism sees human beings as the measure of all things. We have mixed within us the varied and contradictory characteristics of all creation. Judaism does not look on human beings as essentially sinful. *Original sin,* the view of classical Christianity since Paul and Augustine, seems to condemn us to lose the game before we begin. In this view, all human beings are born sinners, and only unearned grace can save them. In the Jewish tradition, each of us writes his or her own personal moral slate. We do not begin life with an unpayable debt. At each moment we make a moral choice. Our lives are the sum of our actions, tempered by our intention, limited by our endowments, ennobled by our faith.

✦ ✦ ✦

It takes work for human society to be orderly, kind, and decent. More than impulse and inspiration, human society needs laws that regulate the complicated interaction of human beings. Our mixed nature, with inclinations to good and evil, needs careful monitoring and specific rules. Judaism is a tradition of law, for it is law—sometimes even when we do not feel like observing it—that preserves society and our own souls.

To be a creature of spirit does not mean casting off law. Spirit, like anything else, requires discipline and work. The master musician must spend agonizing hours practicing uninspiring hand exercises before taking up Brahms; one who would cultivate spirit must realize that discipline and law are the training ground for spirits that seek to climb. Law is the ladder on which an aspiring spirit ascends. Without law allied to our sense of sanctity, the human spirit is unmoored and dangerous.

✦ ✦ ✦

Human beings are hybrid creatures—part angel, part brute. At any moment, we can turn in either direction. What makes being angelic so hard is that part of us will always be brute; what makes being brutish so tragic is that we are granted the possibility of being like angels.

The Challenge of Goodness

The first demand made of a Jew is goodness. Nothing else is more important, no command more central. Tied to the consciousness of God is the need to be good. A verse from the biblical Book of Leviticus reads: "You shall not pick your vineyard bare, or gather the fallen fruit of your vineyard; you shall leave them for the poor and the stranger: I am the Lord your God" (Lev. 19:10). Why is "I am the Lord your God" connected to the command? Because it is a consciousness of God in the world that lets us know that depriving the poor is wrong. We might be tempted to cruelty anyway. But something more than our momentary gain is at stake. The reminder of God's presence brings an awareness of something greater than ourselves, a hope for goodness, for sanctity. In that verse is a reminder that those whom we might seek to abuse are themselves reflections of God.

This philosophy of goodness was unique to Judaism. Before Sinai, people assumed that the gods cared only about sacrifice and prayer. They assumed the gods had the same attitude as selfish human beings, caring only for what could be done to them. In ancient civilizations, from those of the Near East to the Greeks and Romans, human beings were the playthings of the gods, to be used for their divine amusement. Judaism's originality lay in insisting that God cared even more for how we treated other human beings than for how we acted toward God.

Goodness is an acknowledgment of the Divine in another human being and of human fragility. Judaism urges us to sin against God before we would sin against another who is in God's image. God can bear our sin. We cannot injure God, but we can destroy each other. Our first task therefore is kindness toward those who are created in the Divine image: the poor, the stranger, the neighbor, and the friend.

The Torah cautions us about our behavior toward the stranger no less than thirty-six times, because it is often hardest to see God's image in one whom you do not know or understand. Again and again the people of Israel are reminded that they were strangers in the land of Egypt and so must treat the stranger with empathy and decency. Feeling the spark of God in one different from you is at the heart of the Jewish message.

At the root of proper human interaction is a consciousness of the Divine. "You shall be holy for I the Lord your God am holy . . . do not deal falsely with one another" (Lev. 19:1,11). True piety toward God is decency toward God's creations. The first step to holiness is goodness.

After all the fierceness of human history, we have come to understand that being smart or creative or profound will not make one good. Devotees of literature and music and art have done terrible things to their fellow human beings in this world: the murderous commandants of Auschwitz went home and listened to Bach and Mozart. Philosophy alone will not produce goodness: does anyone suppose that professors of ethics are nicer people on average than professors of geology or physics? The only thing that produces goodness is a concentrated, sincere commitment to good acts. "In the beginning," wrote the poet Goethe, "was the deed."

Judaism emphasizes good deeds because nothing else can replace them. To love justice and decency, to hate cruelty and to thirst for righteousness—that is the essence of the human task.

Pleasure and Desire

Why is it so hard to be good?

We are physical creatures with bodies and powerful desires. Religious traditions are often afraid of human appetites. They are afraid because human desire is so unpredictable. A considerate, kind man who for thirty years raised a family runs off with another woman. A caring, careful woman cannot stop herself from gambling away her savings. Why do people succumb to destructive and even vicious impulses? Why do people want things they should not have and pursue those things with such fervor? There are many reasons, some of which we know, some we have yet to discover. Even when we do know, the uncovering of a cause does not always yield solutions. The question for a tradition is not only why but, given our mandate to live together, what should we do?

Different traditions offer distinct answers. Centuries ago, the Buddha decided that desire makes us unhappy. If we did not want, we would not feel frustration and longing. Extinguish desire, destroy all attachment and wanting, and there will be no more unhappiness. He devoted himself to teaching his disciples how to want nothing.

Other traditions, acknowledging the persistence of desire, have tried to blunt or sublimate it. Some counsel minimizing sexuality, for example, or replacing sexual desire with hunger for God. Some made a religion of pleasure itself, counseling that all evil came not from pleasure but from restricting our hedonistic impulses.

Judaism took a different route (although individual Jews have tried all these strategies). One should try neither to wipe out desire nor to redirect it entirely. Pleasure is permitted, even promoted. But Judaism also asks that it be disciplined and sanctified.

What does it mean to control pleasure? "Indulge yourself in all things permitted to you," says the Talmud. Do not shun love. Physical desire and pleasure are a great gift; they are both the pathway to and the expression of deeper intimacy. The very first commandment in the Bible is "be fruitful and multiply." The Jewish tradition does not celebrate the celibate life as an ideal. Like other pleasures, sexuality has the potential to be holy. Desire should not be destroyed; it is part of what makes us human. But our impulses cannot be indiscriminate. We have to channel their expression.

The Jewish encouragement of pleasure extends to almost all areas of life. No observant Jew could be like Mahatma Gandhi, who went on long fasts, sustaining himself on liquids for weeks or months at a time. On the Sabbath, every Jew is commanded to eat three good meals. Dining well is part of celebrating the Sabbath. Food, too, is a gift from God.

Everyone who has ever dieted knows that discipline is a difficult but ultimately rewarding path. The person who decides to eat nothing usually fails, even if the diet briefly succeeds. When we try to refrain from everything good and then *do* fall, we fall heavily. How often do those on a strict diet slip slightly and then watch the whole regimen collapse? The calm, slow wisdom of moderation is the Jewish path. People are not all good or all bad; they are not all body or all soul; their appetites are not constant. A wise life is balanced. Balance has less sparkle than extremism, but balance endures.

The paradox of pleasure is that seeking too much of it brings pain. Gluttony does not multiply the pleasure of food; it destroys it. Controlling pleasure increases it. Judaism helps to channel us into pathways of growth that are steady and permanent. A wise life of spirit is lived in equilibrium. "There is a time," says the Book of Ecclesiastes, "for every purpose under heaven" (Eccl. 3:1).

The Jewish path means living richly and yet being one's own master. Judaism allows us to rejoice in this world, to sample its pleasures, without losing our spiritual center.

Repentance

With its achievements and its anguish, the past is the scaffolding on which our lives are built. In redeeming the past, the future becomes charged with hope. Repentance is the mechanism for rebalancing lives that have been distorted by mistakes or by sin.

We may try to live a life of sanctity, but our own

decisions hinder us. Judaism takes our souls seriously, so it takes our sins seriously. Not every mis-
deed is a sin, but equally, not every sin is a "mistake."
We are in God's image, and just as we celebrate the
nobility of our virtues, we must acknowledge the
gravity of our wrongs. There may be reasons for
them; sometimes they are actions of appetite, sometimes reactions to our anxieties or to our past, but
reasons do not erase responsibility. Even if we blame
our past for what we feel, we can blame only ourselves for what we do.

Yet once a sin has been committed and a soul black-
ened, is there recourse? Words cannot be unspoken,
nor deeds undone. Harm cannot always be repaired.

The heavy weight of misdeeds lies on every feeling
heart. "There is no one so good that he never sins,"
says the Bible in Ecclesiastes (7:20). The certainty of
sin is universal, and the possibility of repair unsure.

Judaism insists we can overcome the past. The Hebrew word *teshuva* means both "turning" and "answer." Turning from sins we have committed, we
answer the persistent question of each soul: How can
I change and unburden myself of my past?

Teshuva means acknowledging one's sin, regretting
it, seeking to repair it, and resolving not to repeat it.
We change the past by making our sins markers to a
new place. Before we had "turned," our sins were

stones on our souls. Now, having done *teshuva*, our transgressions become the catalyst for a renewed self. Each sin becomes a stepping-stone. The past is recast, because it leads to a new place.

To be a faithful Jew means to scour one's soul, seeking to force oneself deeper. *Teshuva* is a hard test; we must not only examine ourselves, we must ask forgiveness from those whom we have hurt. Without confronting those who have suffered by our sins, we cannot do *teshuva*. Repentance must move through us and into the hurt eyes of another human being. We may feel kind and good, but only interchange with others will show if our self-perception is accurate. Without the courage for that confrontation, *teshuva* remains incomplete.

"Though your sins be scarlet, they shall become white as snow" promises the prophet Isaiah (1:18). Sins themselves become transformed when they change our lives. *Teshuva* teaches how to integrate even our sins into the work of art each of us seeks to create from life.

We seek *teshuva* because *in the Jewish tradition the aim of life is to grow in soul.* That is why an old rabbinic saying asserts that a repentant sinner stands upon a height that not even the greatest *tzaddik* (righteous person) can reach. The growth that is required to acknowledge one's sin, to seek to repair it, and to change one's ways is enormous and impressive. With each of those steps, the individual climbs higher and reaches toward holiness.

We sin for many reasons—fear, insensitivity, cruelty, a hunger for pleasure. But true *teshuva* comes not from fear or from the desire for pleasure but from something deeper. True *teshuva* comes from a well-spring of joy. That may sound strange considering the terror and worry and anguish that consciousness of our sins sometimes causes us. But the end of a soul aligned with itself, with others, and with God is a feeling of great joy. The reward of sin is immediate and obvious, otherwise we would not sin. The reward of *teshuva* is gradual but lasting.

Teshuva is the soul's homecoming in this world. The pain of sin has been transfigured to joy, and the past has become a path back to God.

Joy

Deeper than pleasure is joy. Joy is a satisfaction of the soul, a combination of gratitude, safety, and calm exultation. Growing in soul enables us to taste joy.

There are those who, knowing little of Judaism, believe it is a tradition of suffering, guilt, and unrelieved remorse. But constant mourning is the sign of an ailing soul, one that needs healing. Joy is the natural condition of a human being relating to the Creator of the universe. Judaism is not a tradition of tragedy, and all the dire events of Jewish history have not changed its core of joy.

"Worship God in gladness" writes the Psalmist (Ps. 100:2). That advice was echoed powerfully by the later Jewish tradition. Most of the prayers and songs of the Jewish tradition were written with joy and are offered up with hopeful and trusting hearts. Judaism has seen more than its share of calamity, and anyone could excuse generations of Jews if their world view was morose and pessimistic. Yet for all the expressions of pain and sorrow that exist in such abundance in the Jewish tradition, the prevailing view is found in the words of a talmudic Rabbi: "There is no sadness in the presence of God."

A Live Mind

A paradox of joy is that it cannot be had by seeking. One who schemes to be joyous ends up depressed and empty. But for human beings, happiness often results from a full and challenging use of the gifts we are given. In Judaism no gift is taken more seriously or exercised more strenuously than that of the human capacity for imagination and thought.

Judaism is a tradition with profound respect for the

human mind. All religious traditions tell stories and legends about God, and these reflect their own scale of values. Judaism tells tales of God studying.

Jews are one quarter of 1 percent of the world population. Yet they make up almost 30 percent of the world's Nobel Prize winners. Such achievement is not bred in the genes. It is a product of centuries of insistence on the gift of the human mind. The great heroes of Jewish spirituality always include scholars and sages.

Made in the image of God, we are obligated to cultivate and not neglect the great gifts we are given. The human mind is first among the marvels of this world. From a small room, it can comprehend the constellations thousands of light-years away; it can make marks on a page that will inspire other minds centuries later; it can spin stories and create equations; it can plot and muse and hope and realize frenzied dreams. What person who understands the blessing he or she was given would ever disdain it?

Judaism also encourages study, because while the problems of life are new to each individual, they are not new to humanity as a whole. All the deep dilemmas we will face in our lives have been faced before, and others can help us understand how to meet them. For almost four thousand years the Jewish tradition has grappled with the most difficult questions of life—questions of relationships, of families, of illness and death, of dreams delayed and lives unful-filled, of making success meaningful, of living with others, of living with loneliness. No human problem is new or alien to Judaism. Within its texts and teach-ings lie thousands of years of wise guidance.

Sometimes our answer may be different from those of our ancestors. Our world has changed in many ways. But human nature has not changed. Our trag-edies and joys beat inside of us as they did in the hearts of those who went before. If we listen to their stories, our own paths can be made smoother and kinder.

Why do Jews place such value on study? Because in the Jewish tradition, God was revealed through words. We can glimpse God in other human beings, in the marvels of the world, and in the depths of one's own soul, but what shaped the history of Judaism was a book. Judaism is an astonishing testimony to the magical power of words, transmitted through genera-tions, to alter lives and change history.

Shaping a Self

We are too arrogant and too humble. We pride our-selves on things for which we deserve no credit: our intellect, our appearance, our natural endowments.

We arrogantly claim praise for gifts we were simply lucky to have received.

Yet we are too humble in dodging responsibility for our own behavior. We claim that our circumstances alone created us, but such insistence is almost always heard when we have done something wrong, not something praiseworthy. Do well, and it is our merit; fail, and curse fate.

"Everything," says the Talmud, "is in the hands of heaven except the awe of heaven." It is true: we do not create our circumstances in this world, but we do fashion our response. Each individual crafts the moral story of his or her life. The clay is given; the shape of the sculpture is ours. Against our will, notes the Talmud, we are born; against our will, we die. But the tale told within those brackets is not fated. Ability is inherited, but a self is formed from choice, from effort, and from faith.

More than anything else, we shape ourselves through our deeds. Most modern advice does not take realizing ourselves through deeds very seriously. We are besieged by books and lectures on how to make ourselves happy, rich, and self-realized. The authors promise great deeds will follow once we are properly attuned. Deed will follow enlightenment.

But focusing on the self alone can be spiritually deadening. To grow in soul is not only to plunge inside ourselves. We do not always need to be filled up inside in order to give; sometimes it is in the act of giving that we are filled up. Spirit contradicts the laws of physics: in being expended, it grows greater.

Large spirits grow larger through love, and love is real only through deed. A love that is only feeling, that stays inside, becomes a solitary entanglement of soul. True love involves an *expression* of emotion, an outpouring of soul. For in focusing on others, we are returned to our deeper selves. Like all deep acts, love teaches us about ourselves in the process of caring for and serving the other.

Judaism does teach how to explore the self through prayer and meditation and introspection. But it is primarily a faith of deed. For the world needs more than our self-exploration. It needs our action. Sometimes it may seem that action takes away from a focus on our own souls, but at times the only true way to find ourselves is by not seeking.

Courage

Living as a Jew means being different, and being different takes courage. But there is no training for the soul that is as important and as bracing as a schooling in courage.

Taking faith seriously means that it will touch you and change your life. That is threatening, both to our own complacency and to the settled attitudes of those who know us. We are told our faith is not supposed to be "too serious." But religion that does not touch our lives is a hobby, not a faith. How can we take the ultimate questions of life lightly? Faith and fate and destiny need not be solemn—few traditions are as hospitable to humor as Judaism—but they are serious.

What if Judaism begins to seep into your soul? What will others think of you? The answer will vary, but some will be dismayed. Many will not understand. Some will respect your conviction and recognize the courage required to take a stand of enlightened faith in our age, in our land.

Whatever reactions you encounter, one conclusion is clear: it is a foolish life that is lived in the minds of others. The attempt to fine-tune the perception of others is draining and futile. Ultimately, inside our own souls we know if we have lived with courage or cowardice. Let others choose for themselves.

To live as a Jew is to cast your destiny with a numerically small people, a people that is no stranger to change or challenge or disdain. It is a people that has long realized that the opinion of others cannot always be relied upon and that ultimately only the bearer of a soul can know its secret workings.

If you live in this world and are not merely passing through it, you will have to listen to what stirs your soul. The journey itself—exhausting, exhilarating, and wondrous—will begin to enchant you, and courage will carry you past the objections of those who will not understand.

When God called to Abraham, Abraham responded with a single word, *hineni*—''Here I am.''

· 2 ·

TO JOIN A PEOPLE

It is not because you are the most numerous
of peoples that I have set my heart upon you and
treasured you—indeed, you are the fewest.
Deuteronomy 7:7

You Are the Fewest

For much of their history, the Jews have been a small, beleaguered people. To live as a Jew is a double statement of faith. It presumes a belief not only in God but in the resilience and importance of the Jewish people.

The first mention of Jews in history, outside the Bible, is in a small stone tablet called the stele of Mernpetah. It is a fragment of an Egyptian record dating from about the twelfth century B.C.E.—over three thousand years ago. It reads "Israel is laid waste —his seed is no more." The very first allusion to Jews in history boasts that they are destroyed.

Today, both Jews and Judaism survive. They survive as more than a religion: Jews are a people. One is born into or joins the Jewish people. To live as a Jew is to grieve with the sorrows of other Jews and to rejoice in their triumphs. To be a Jew is to cast one's lot with this small, remarkable family of faith.

The Jewish People

The Jewish people might have left no trace in history. Beginning in the pagan city of some ancient visionary, they were no different than thousands of other ragged tribes who went before and came after them. They began as a tiny clan and managed somehow to survive as a nation. Even so, their mark might have been slight. They were slaves and conquerors, sometimes noble, sometimes cruel and bloody. Any history book chronicles many such nations who briefly streaked across the skies of the past and are no more.

But the Jews changed history. Strangely enough, almost four thousand years after that first visionary, this tiny tribe of people still stands at the center stage of history.

Jews are not special because of inherent qualities. There is no Jewish "race"—thousands of years of mixing, conversion, and wandering have produced a mingled and varied gene pool. Jews are found in every racial group in the world. Jewish destiny is not bred in the genes.

Jewish destiny is a function of memory and vision. What the Jewish people *does* have is a tradition, message, and a mission. The vast accomplishments of Jews were built upon that past. Without a continual commitment to the tradition and aims of Judaism, to its moral and spiritual ideals, Jews will ultimately be indistinguishable from others; even more, without a thriving Judaism, Jews will simply disappear.

How long will Jews distinguish themselves in the sciences, the arts, politics, and philosophy? In our age, Jews have made remarkable contributions to culture. Yet many have done so while ignoring or disregarding their heritage. If Jews abandon the mission and message of Judaism, the radiance will fade. Achievement cannot long outlive the culture and beliefs that nurtured it. The greatest Jewish thinkers and artists in our time are a generation or two away from the Rabbis and talmudic academies. Although many are increasingly ignorant of the Jewish tradition, Jewish heritage and history still help shape their outlook and drive their accomplishments. Classical Jewish texts and ancient tales have not lost their power to shape values and focus minds. The tradition carries within itself the seeds of creativity and accomplishment. Yet what will happen in another generation or two should the ideals and aims of Judaism fade altogether?

The Jewish philosopher Will Herberg once spoke of "cut-flower ethics." He argued that Jewish ethical norms will last for a brief while, even apart from Jewish teachings, just as flowers uprooted from the soil stay in bloom for a short time after cutting. But soon the flowers fade. Behaviors, too, disintegrate if cut from the soil in which they were nourished. All those teachers and scientists and musicians and artists are the bloom of Jewish spirituality; given time, without the soil, that bloom will fade.

However, Judaism is far more than a vehicle to success in any given field. Keeping the tradition alive also keeps alive the connection to other Jews. For thousands of years, Jews have responded when other Jews cried out. At a time when the Soviet Union oppressed all religions alike, it was Jews who clamored for the release of their brothers and sisters; at a time when civil war was ravaging Ethiopia, it was Jews who airlifted their brethren out of that war-scarred land. Bound together by an extraordinary history and a promised destiny, Jews could not turn away. And in the process of rescuing their kin, Jews turned the world's attention to the plight of others as well. In the end, thousands of Ethiopians and countless Soviets were saved. For the Jewish people, forgetting is a

sin, and to ignore the suffering of others is to forsake
the overwhelming lessons of Jewish history.

The Jewish people wandered throughout most of
their history, a fate decreed not by a malicious God
but by a hostile humanity. Yet wherever a Jew wandered, somewhere in the far reaches of his dispersion
there would be another Jew, willing to take him in, to
care for him, to worship with him. "All of Israel is
responsible for one another." That simple creed was
the lifeline of a people often cast out by the world.
The sense of mutual responsibility forced Jews to
think beyond the boundary of individual needs to
something greater: to the history and destiny of a people. It created the bonds of international family that
again and again saved not only individual Jews but
the Jewish people as a whole. To be part of a Jewish
community is to be taken in, succored, and even
saved by a commitment that runs deeper than history,
a commitment that grows out of the covenant of the
Jewish people.

Chosenness and the Jewish Mission

"Never doubt that a small group of concerned people
can change the world," Margaret Mead once said.
"Indeed, it is the only thing that ever has." Judaism
is about changing the world. That statement would

seem too grand, even absurd, if history did not show that Judaism has indeed changed the world.

The Jewish people came out of Egypt bearing a message and a mission. The message was the highest truth—of one God, a God who cares for human beings and who is passionately concerned about what we do. The mission was to bring the world to recognize that highest truth.

Judaism is a system for realizing that truth in the world. God is not something we can know. But a relationship with God is something we can develop, and godly action, something we can achieve. We reach God in spiritual search and in moral behavior. Judaism teaches both. That is its mission and its message.

With that simple message, whose depth embraces lifetimes of learning, Judaism presents itself to humanity and to each searching soul.

Living a Jewish life means joining a cause that is greater than ourselves. It means contributing to the betterment of the world, what some in the Jewish tradition have called *tikkun olam* (repairing the world). It means taking the secret of our soul and joining it to others who believe in redeeming the world through goodness and spiritual passion.

This idea of mission is at the heart of the concept of chosenness. Judaism was chosen to teach Judaism, to teach the realization of and the path to one God. To be chosen is not to be better than others; it is to be called to be better than one currently is. To be chosen is to have a mission to improve the world and to feel that when we slight that task or abandon it, we are reneging on our deep purpose.

The *brit,* or covenant, is the acceptance by the Jewish people of that mission. The covenant is a contract with God to represent a certain ideal and way of life in this world. Covenant lies at the heart of Jewish self-definition—a sense that Judaism is a vital part of the progress of human history and moral growth and that Jews should devote themselves to learning and living that system.

There have been times of persecution and difficulty when Jews, powerless and besieged, have interpreted chosenness as meaning that they are better than those who victimize them. But that is the message of chosenness disfigured by the ugliness of history. And even under such conditions, unlike other traditions, Judaism did not insist that only its adherents could be saved or that only Jews were under the care of Providence. In the face of a world that often told them they had to convert to Christianity in order to be saved, Judaism declared, in the words of the Rabbis, that "the righteous of *all* nations have a share in the world to come." So Jewish chosenness was actually *less* exclusive than the chosenness characteristic of many other peoples and faiths.

Today the Jewish mission is not diminished. In a world that still cries out for healing, where suffering and narrowness are endemic, to be chosen means to have a special calling to teach that all human beings are children of God created in God's image and must be treated as sacred.

That Judaism is a small nation is no bar to this task. Many of the nations that have changed the world have been small: the Athens of Socrates and Plato, the England of Queen Elizabeth and Shakespeare, the America of Washington and Jefferson. No nation, great or small, has touched humanity more deeply than the tiny nation of Isaiah and Jeremiah.

Chosenness in the Jewish tradition is not a privilege to boast of but a task to be undertaken. It is to keep constantly in mind the words of the prophet Micah: "God has declared, O Man, what is good and what the Lord requires of you—to do justice, to love mercy, and to walk humbly with your God" (Mic. 6:8).

The Land of Israel

In the Bible, God promises Abraham two things: a people and a land. The promise of a people is clear, for only with a group can a tradition and a mission be realized. Abraham's descendants will be God's "shock

troops"—the ones who will bring a message of mono-
theism to the ancient pagan world.

But the promise of a land is equally important. A
land is what permits a people to function *in this world.*
A land is the gathering point, the place to learn and
test the lessons of the message.

So Abraham begins the journey to Israel. For centuries Jews set up their state in that small land and
sought to create a society in which the messages of
their tradition were heard. In some ages they suc-
ceeded; in others, they failed. Eventually the land of
Israel was conquered and the Jews dispersed. Although in the end Judaism spread its message around
the world, it never forgot that the ultimate challenge
was to live and create in its own land.

The story of the land of Israel is one of the most
remarkable that history has to offer. Beginning more
than three thousand years ago, Jews set up a state in
Israel that lasted for some five hundred years, over
twice the current age of the United States. The state
was eventually destroyed, and the Jews were dispersed. The Northern Kingdom was overrun in 722
B.C.E., and the Southern Kingdom, in 586 B.C.E., when
the Temple in Jerusalem was destroyed. But a century later, many Jews returned and renewed the
state, until the first century of the common era when
it was once again—and seemingly for all time—
wiped out.

Eighteen hundred years passed. Jews, scattered over the globe, dreamed of an impossible return to Israel. From all the lands of their dispersion, Jewish eyes were turned toward Israel. In their prayers, Jews prayed for a return to Zion, to Jerusalem, to the time when they had control over their own destiny. In their prayers, they prayed for the fertility of the land, that it should receive rain in its season, that the hills should be green and the valleys verdant. All of this remained part of the liturgy of the Jewish people, even among those whose families had not seen Israel for a thousand years.

In the last century, a group of wild dreamers and visionaries emerged from this powerless people. They began to plot a return to their ancestral land. Then through a combination of courage, persuasiveness, persistence, and the sympathy of the world following the Holocaust, the Jews returned.

The return has itself been filled with trial and pain. Surrounded by hostile nations, Israel's first decades of existence were filled with tension and war. As the Israeli writer David Grossman has said, "In the land of the Jews, before our children learn the facts of life, they learn the facts of death." Despite the difficulties, the land of Israel is in many ways the most astounding realization of vision in modern history.

Israel is a land with many problems and moral challenges. Yet we who dwell at a comfortable distance must recall the following: Israel exists in a region where there is no other democracy; it was built primarily by people who themselves had no experience of democracy, having come from the totalitarian, authoritarian, and/or tyrannical regimes of Eastern Europe and the Middle East. Since its inception, it has been plunged into constant war. It is itself a tiny nation, about the size of Rhode Island, surrounded for more than forty years by hostile countries who together total an area far larger than the United States; and despite all this, it is a thriving democracy. That is more than a miracle of statecraft. It is a tribute to the moral legacy of Judaism.

Israel is the spiritual center of the Jewish people. In that tiny land is the only permanent home the Jews have managed to find. Israel is home in the classic definition of the poet Robert Frost: "Home is the place where, when you have to go there, they have to take you in." Every other country can accept or reject Jews in trouble. The history of Jewish refugees seeking sanctuary among the nations of the world has often been one of frustration, denial, and tragedy. Israel has always committed itself to taking them in; Israel is their home.

In the mid-1980s, when the first Ethiopian Jews were brought to Israel, I was in Jerusalem. Like many in Israel at the time, I was riveted by the news. One day I was listening to a broadcast on the British

Broadcasting Corporation foreign service. The first planeloads of Ethiopian Jews had just arrived. I shall never forget the commentator's words. "I have never been too sympathetic to the policies and ideology of Israel," he said. "But I must say this. No other nation on the globe—or in history—would have sent its soldiers halfway across the world to rescue people of another race and a different culture because they said, 'We are your brothers and sisters.'"

In that simple declaration is summed up the spirit of Israel. It is not a perfect land, for there are no perfect people. But it is the place that has always stood at the center of Jewish fate, and in its history-soaked hills is the memory and much of the meaning of the Jewish journey.

Torah and Tradition

How did the Jewish people endure all the years they were *not* in their land? Though scores of persecuted nations have vanished, some would have us believe that Jews have survived *because* they were persecuted. But being hated does not ensure survival any more than being thrown into a lake ensures one can swim; it can be a dramatic demonstration of the skill, but some deeper resource must already exist, or a person will drown, a people disappear.

The survival of Judaism is both more obvious and more enigmatic. One thing we *can* say is that it begins with a book. The Jewish people treasured their sacred book, the Torah. From its text they spun endless commentaries, digests, laws, psychological insights, remedies, prophecies, and dreams. In this single sacred book lies the key to Jewish survival: the concept of God and moral duty that the Jews introduced to the world.

The pivotal moment of Jewish history came after centuries of slavery in Egypt. At the foot of Mount Sinai, this newly freed people, bewildered and frightened, were charged with their mission. As slaves, their object had been merely to survive. *As a nation,* their object would be to proclaim the highest purpose of life: that humanity should reach beyond survival and even comfort to a life of holiness.

For millennia Jewish philosophers and writers have elaborated that insight. Some have seen the Torah as the literal word of God, given in the desert verbatim as it is written in the Hebrew Bible today. Others have seen the Bible as a book written by human beings under Divine inspiration or encouragement. Whatever the origin, for centuries people have worked to expand and explain the wisdom symbolized by that moment at the mountain. Today Judaism is a vast system, but it all spins around the axis of Sinai.

Sinai is more than a geographical place; it is a powerful spiritual symbol. How does one absorb the messages of the Torah? The Rabbis made it very clear: "To learn Torah one must make oneself open like the desert." To grasp the Torah and its teachings cannot be simply a process of intellectual understanding; rather it must seep into one's soul. The desert mountain of Sinai represents the place where the Jewish spirit reached up to attain the teachings of Torah.

The Torah has been for Jews the boundless book of life—a book of inspiration, instruction, argument, delight, confusion, enlightenment. There is a tradition of constant interpretation that reflects the new insights and disciplines of each age. "Turn it over and over," urges one talmudic Rabbi, "for everything is in it."

"Everything" is the understandable hyperbole of a Rabbi in love with the source of sacred teaching. The Torah does not contain all the world's information or even every laudable moral teaching. But it is astonishing how in each age seemingly new theories and ideas are seen to have their antecedents in the Torah and in the elaboration of the Torah by the rabbis of the Talmud. The study of Torah is constantly evolving: in modern times, literary analysis, archaeological evaluation, historical comparison, and other trends have gained favor. But the Torah itself refuses to yield all its secrets. Ultimately it is, as the theologian Heschel has written, a record of how God and human beings seek each other in this world. It is the timeless chronicle of that never-ending search, with moments of closeness and estrangement, triumph and anguish.

Does the Torah really have the kind of power this description suggests? Until the collapse of the Soviet Union, Jews who traveled there would try to smuggle in copies of the Torah, hidden in old clothes or secret luggage compartments. It had to be smuggled in because this ancient book was banned. Why did the Soviet Union, one of the two most powerful nations on earth, fear the words of this old Hebrew text? Because as the Torah itself teaches, its words are fire, and they can sear a soul. Even superpowers cannot control the force of words that can kindle souls. Sometimes tributes come from unlikely places; the fear of the Soviet censors was a paradoxical tribute to the continuing power of the sacred word.

To be a Jew means to be an inheritor of the Torah, whose teachings profoundly changed the world. It is to be a student of the Torah, whose teachings, each day, continue to change lives.

Hatred and the Holocaust

Hatred of the Jewish people is one of the most heinous, persistent strains of history. Though fed by many streams, including theological myths, economic fears, political calculation, and pure hatred of difference, no explanation is sufficient. The hatred is pure because it is truly based upon nothing—its origin lies not in reason, but in murky, irrational fears.

Anti-Semites* will always give a reason. Jews have been hated for being assimilationists, separatists, communists, capitalists, chosen, discarded, scattered and homeless, nationalist and banded together, for being weak and for being strong. Any excuse will serve the hater.

Hatred of Jews peaked but sadly did not end with the Holocaust. In that unimaginable conflagration, called in Hebrew the *shoah* (whirlwind), one third of all the Jews in the world were killed. The *shoah* began in one of the most progressive societies in the world at that time—Germany. It was not only another proof of the virulence of anti-Semitism, but it destroyed what remained of the easy faith humanity had in its own progress and enlightenment. Clearly there remained dark, violent, horrid forces inside of human beings. Once again, it was the figure of the Jews upon whom those forces were vented.

---

* *Anti-Semite* is really a euphemism for "Jew hater." The word is the invention of Wilhelm Marr, a nineteenth-century anti-Semite who was looking for a term that would offer more scientific respectability than *Jew hater*.

That Jews have been hated, hunted, beleaguered, and often alone is no reason to be Jewish. That the Nazis sought to destroy not only Jews, but Judaism, is no reason to be Jewish. Evil people have sought to wipe out many things; that alone does not obligate us to keep those things alive.

But that in the face of such millennial persecution, in the face of the torturer, the murderer, the hater, the Jew should remain Jewish—that is something worth pondering. Even the death camps could not extinguish the religious devotion of the Jewish people. In the camps themselves, many prayed, observed what and when they could, found courage and solace in ancient teachings, keeping holiness of spirit alive in the midst of hell. More powerful than the haters is the love of the Jews for their own tradition, a love that did not fail even in the face of the most grievous sufferings.

To suffer is neither shaming nor ennobling. It is simply terrible and tragic. Yet how one reacts to suffering is often the critical test of character. The dignity of Jewish suffering comes not from the suffering itself but from the resolution of Jews in the face of horror, generation after generation: that through such times Jews still created, still learned and thrived and loved; that is a remarkable achievement.

The story of Jewish suffering is in a deep sense not about the Jews but about the haters. Generations of persecution teach us that humanity is at times a savage species, and we need constantly to remind ourselves of the human capacity for evil. Those of us who live in a relatively safe world would like to turn away from such horror, but Judaism insists that upon memory, even memory that is painful, hangs the only hope of redemption. Judaism well understood the lesson of modern psychology that it is the unremembered past that is most dangerous. What we remember we can place in perspective. But those who cannot confront their past will be enslaved to it.

Judaism insists upon retelling the story of its suffering. Judaism tells the story first because the persecution and pain of others should be honored and remembered, and it tells the story because we can learn from their resolution in the face of evil: by remembering, we can appreciate and overcome. The first thing a Jewish child learns, sitting at the Passover seder, is that her ancestors were born into bondage. That is a lesson in the hatred of enslavement and the appreciation of freedom.

Not the way Jews died but rather the way they lived should claim our allegiance. When we read about the millions who lost their lives in the *shoah,* are we touched by their stories and their dreams? Do we grieve for the loss of what they might have been? Are we captivated by what one poet called the "mutilated music" of their lives?

We remember the haters not only for what they did but for what they could not do: they could not crush the vitality of the Jewish spirit or destroy the religious vigor of the Jewish people.

We also remember the haters because they are not gone. And until the human heart is cleansed, we must guard against its darkness.

Mostly we remember the innocent. Their courage, their learning, their devotion in the midst of the flame, touch our hearts and persuade us to use our lives in part to honor them and their ideals. The ultimate and appropriate way to avenge their murders is to allow the victims to live on not only in memory but in our lives.

The Hero

If you wish to know the character of a people, look to its heroes.

The classical heroes of the Jewish tradition are moral heroes. The Bible tells of leaders who were successful in administration and even in conquest but who, because of their own characters, were disregarded or even derided. They were not heroes.

Still, heroes in the Jewish tradition are people with all the flaws of normal human beings. Scrolling down the rolls of Jewish heroes, none escapes fault. The

Bible does not whitewash its champions. We are told of the sins of Abraham, Sarah, Moses, Miriam, David, and Esther; we know of their fears and reluctance but also of their courage and resolution. We read about their distance from God and their reconciliations. In the end, moral striving is what counts, not perfection.

The quintessential Jewish hero in the Bible is the prophet. Hebrew prophets do not foretell the future; rather, they see deeply into the present. The prophet recognizes the evil and corruption of society and warns, in ringing tones, of what will happen if it persists. The prophet defends the ideals of God against the iniquity of the people.

Again and again in the Bible, the prophet also defends the people against the judgments of God. For the prophet is not only animated by a yearning for justice; the prophet is moved by love. There is both anger and love in the prophet's stern warnings not to oppress the widow and the orphan, to care for the poor, the dispossessed, the bereaved and alone. The prophet carries inside both love of God and love of humanity. Such a capacity for love, coupled with a thirst for justice, makes a hero in Judaism.

The prophet is not detached from society. Unlike the heroes of some other traditions, the prophet is in the marketplace, among the people, haranguing and scolding, encouraging and dreaming together with the nation. It is not enough to love humanity in the abstract but disdain dealing with real people. The prophet can be gentle or cutting but never distant.

The Jewish people have raised not only prophets but sages, scholars, and some political leaders to the status of heroes. Traditionally, neither physical prowess nor artistic skill was enough. The most physically powerful of all biblical heroes, Samson, is a figure of fun, one who only redeems his frivolous life by a final courageous act. And even skill with words, even the skill of prophecy, are not guarantors of status. In the Torah the great pagan prophet Bilaam is condemned because he sells his prophetic skills. Despite his gifts, Bilaam is driven by personal concern and not ethical ardor.

Modern society tends to be skeptical of heroes, because we have made heroes of those who are simply skillful or attractive. When they disappoint us, we discard them. There will always be another, a hero whose merit is of the moment, who will capture our hearts for a season. But Judaism does not see beauty or charm or athleticism as enough to make a hero. And it acknowledges that all heroes have flaws; indeed, that struggling with imperfection is one of the components of heroism.

The classical medieval code of Jewish law, the Shulchan Aruch (The Set Table) opens by declaring that one should arise "as a hero" each morning to do the will of God. Heroism is realizing the highest

potentials within us. Skill, talent, magnetism, cha-
risma—these are all morally neutral. No one is a hero
for being born with certain talents. One is only a hero
for using one's gifts in ways that improve the world.
There is an everyday heroism that comes from the
attempt, in normal life situations, to do what is good
and what is right. Not only grand historical figures are
heroes. The Jewish tradition also sees as heroic those
who strive continually to improve the world in small
incremental ways, in acts of everyday goodness.

Conversion: Choosing Judaism

Judaism has always enunciated a message to the
world. To appreciate that message, however, one did
not have to become Jewish. At times Judaism was
more vigorous in seeking converts, at other times less
so. When in the early centuries of the common era,
the Christian government of Rome made it punish-
able by death to convert to Judaism, the practice of
soliciting conversions died out, and the Jewish attitude toward converts became at times prickly and sus-
picious.

Traditionally, however, Judaism was pleased and
proud to accept converts. The Talmud states, "A convert is dearer to God even than the Israelites who
stand at the mountain of Sinai."

That deep tradition of welcoming those who choose Judaism has been renewed in our own day. Judaism has once again begun to benefit from the infusion of many people who are in search of a meaningful path of life. Of course there are many different motivations for converting. Among converts are those who are moved by Judaism's beliefs and ideals. Others convert to marry a Jew.

Conversion for marriage is sometimes frowned upon. Yet it is in many ways an ideal reason to convert, for it is a statement of eagerness to join the Jewish people. Intellectual conviction alone is a fragile thing; another argument, a new book, and one may be dissuaded. But belonging to a family is powerful, and many people come to tradition through the avenue of association.

Indeed the prototypical convert in the Bible, in the Book of Ruth, is motivated by family ties, not by ideology. Ruth converts after the deaths of her husband and father-in-law, when her mother-in-law, Naomi, decides to return to Israel. Ruth has grown very attached to Naomi and does not wish to abandon her. So she declares in a beautiful passage: "Wherever you go, I will go; wherever you lodge, I will lodge; your people shall be my people, and your God my God" (Ruth 1:16). Notice that for Ruth "your people shall be my people" comes first. Often, theology follows love for another person and the joining of a new family.

For make no mistake: in becoming Jewish, one joins not just a religion but a people. Even Jews who do not have strong religious convictions or *any* religious convictions can feel strongly about their identity as Jews, because Judaism is broader than any statement of faith. It is a civilization, a culture—ultimately, a sort of national family. Without a center of spirit, that national family will not survive, but it remains true that whatever one's spiritual commitments, joining Judaism is also automatically joining Jews.

In our day, Jews must and should welcome those who would cast their fate with us. Some of the most talented and dedicated Jews in the world are those who were not born Jewish. Judaism is not a race but a spiritual inheritance, and the Talmud ascribes a special merit in those who were not themselves born Jewish but who share its ideals and are moved by the rhythms of its law and lore.

The Ever-Dying People

Sometimes accident or illness brings us face-to-face with our own mortality. An individual who has confronted his or her mortality lives differently thereafter; often this individual is left with a surer sense of what is important and a keener recognition that life's precious thread could snap at any moment.

Has any people faced its own mortality as often as the Jews? Again and again it has seemed to Jews of a given era that they were the last of their kind. Their laments fill the pages of Jewish history, from the biblical cries of exile and destruction to the heartrending dirge of the poet Yitzhak Katzenelson in the wake of the Holocaust in *Song of the Murdered Jewish People:* "Woe is unto me, nobody is left. . . . There was a people and it is no more. There was a people and it is. . . . Gone."

The Jewish philosopher Simon Rawidowicz once wrote an essay titled "Israel: The Ever Dying People." He gathered examples of Jewish writing throughout history that proclaimed the end of Jewry. Each generation, Rawidowicz asserted, has its own version of anxiety about being the last bearers of the tradition.

Jews have repeatedly confronted the possibility of their own destruction. Such an experience cannot help but leave its imprint on the Jewish psyche. One of the consequences is a hair-trigger sensitivity to any hint of threat; but this is not the deepest reaction.

The deepest reaction that Judaism has in the face of its own end is paradoxical: a love of this life combined with an awareness of its fragility. One should hold fast to life but hold fast knowing that no grip ultimately will suffice, that however sure one's grasp, it may at any moment falter.

The great Hasidic Rabbi Nachman of Bratslav summed it up in a widely quoted epigram that became a popular Hebrew song: "All of the world is a very narrow bridge, and the most important thing is not to fear at all."

Jews have walked along that narrow bridge for almost four thousand years, and much of the time they have gazed over the side at the abyss. It was never too far from their feet. The result did not create fear alone, though the Jews have certainly not always escaped fear. Rather, those gazers at the abyss developed a love of the bridge itself, of the narrow path that the living walk. It is love of life, its complexity, its rich surprises, its beauty and awesome terror, that have kept the Jewish people creative and flourishing. In culture after culture they have created new worlds: the talmudic world of the Rabbis; the legends of the storytellers; the poetry of Hebrew bards; the kabbalah of the medieval mystics; the magic ecstasy of the Hasidim; the researches of modern scholars and the new customs of contemporary seekers. In all these and more, the law, history, tradition, folklore, food, humor, dance, music, and prayer were expressions of an enchantment with this world. Jews felt themselves, and feel themselves still, dancing on the bridge. But the burden of Jewish history does not slow the dance. For the dancers are moved by an infatuation with the lushness of God's world and a fascination with the puzzles and mysteries that have yet to be resolved. At times when Judaism is gripped by that love, Jews do not fear.

That is part of the secret. That is part of the reason why the ever-dying people will not die.

· 3 ·

TO SEEK GOD

I sing hymns and weave songs
because my soul yearns for You.
Shir HaKavod

What Is God?

To ask the question What is God? is to realize the shortcomings of our language and the limitations of our intellects. We can no more grasp God than a newborn can understand physics. On one level, all inquiry is useless. All that we can say about God is what the medieval Jewish philosopher Joseph Albo said: To truly understand God, one would have to be God. No other being is great enough to fathom the Divine.

But no religious tradition has been willing to stop with that declaration. For though our minds may not be able to grasp the greatness of God, we human beings must make our way in *this* world, and declara-

61

tions of ignorance do not carry us very far. So humanity has speculated, imagined, dreamed, written poetry and theology, told stories, and prayed to something we cannot truly understand. For though we cannot understand God, and all our statements about God are too simple, too fragmentary, too *human* to embrace the Divine, the need to speak about such an overwhelming reality does not abate. So once again, drawing on our traditions, humanity turns its collective eye toward the heavens and addresses the infinite.

Talking About God

How do we speak about God? Many of the mystics have recommended silence. In the magic enveloping soundlessness, our consciousness is freed. Nothing traps us, limits us, forces us to hang on to this concept or that word. The Psalmist writes, "Silence is fitting praise for you" (Ps. 65:2). The moment we begin to speak we are trapped by our language.

Almost any word we use in relation to God is problematic. Even *merciful* or *loving* are words that apply to human beings. What can it really mean to talk this way about something so far beyond our grasp?

We see this limitation in the much-discussed prob-

lem of gender language with relation to God. The
problem of God and gender is a limitation not of God
but of human speech. To call God "He" is no more
accurate or inaccurate than to call God "She." In
the Jewish tradition, God has no body, no gender,
cannot be described the way we describe our neigh-
bors and friends. This book avoids pronouns in refer-
ring to God except when quoting. When this makes
syntax awkward, we are reminded that language can
be clumsy and obstructive as well as graceful and
clarifying.

Tactics like avoiding personal pronouns remind us
that God is ineffable—beyond conception or description. Perhaps silence can help us in the recesses of
our own minds. But silence cannot be shared *exactly*,
and for us the world is given shape by words. So
unless we are willing to remain silent, we must take
the risk of speaking about God.

We have a good precedent. Throughout history, religious traditions have spoken about this reality that is
beyond words. In Judaism, the Torah, the Talmud,
and the medieval philosophers have talked a great
deal about God. Sometimes it seems they are describ-
ing a human being, using human metaphors like
"God sees" or "God's love" or "God's right hand."
The Talmud's explanation for this is that "the Torah
speaks in the language of human beings." We have

no "Divine language" that would allow us accurately to portray that which we cannot grasp. So long as we are human, we cannot escape human language.

It is our task, however, to remember that all we are saying is limited by our language. As one prayer puts it, "Were the skies made of parchment, all the reeds quills, all the seas and waters made of ink, and every inhabitant of earth a scribe," we still could not begin to do justice to God's nature.

God may be far beyond our power of imagination, but imagination itself is a gift of God, as is the faculty of speech, the reach of mind, and the yearnings of our souls. If we seek to describe what is beyond us, it is because the endowments we have been given will not allow us to rest without giving utterance to our curiosity, our reverence, and our hope.

The God of the Rabbis

God is the great creative force of the universe and is ready to enter into a relationship with each human being. Those two ideas, so far away from each other, together make up the heart of the traditional Jewish notion of God. God is infinitely far away and excruciatingly close; God is the shaper of galaxies and a source of guidance and love in the life of the lowliest among us who are ticking off our days tucked into a corner of the cosmos on this small spinning planet.

God as understood by the Rabbis of the Talmud is a God who is involved in human life, who cares for the fate of creation, who has given us a sense of how life ought to be lived.

The essence of the rabbinic conception of God has less to do with what God is than with how human beings and God draw close. For ideally the relationship between God and human beings is a relationship of law and of love.

Law is the skeleton of behavior, of conduct that governs our lives. Law provides the framework. And love provides the force.

Judaism tries to bring us to that love through action. For the Rabbis of the Talmud, each moment, each act, was infused with a sense of God's love and of an individual's love for God. God was most obvious in that which was so often overlooked: the simple existence of the world, the gift of life, the powers of human beings to think, to cherish, to notice and adore—all of these are manifestations of God's love.

We are trained to think of God as something to be addressed at prescribed times—when we step into a house of prayer, when we are in trouble, or perhaps in moments of celebration. But for the Rabbis, God was ever present. The path of faith is to find God not only in special moments but in each moment. For by finding God in them, each moment was made special.

Where did the Rabbis look for God's presence? In everything. The Bible depicts the world as filled with the glory of God, and the Rabbis took that biblical assurance to heart. God was found in the thornbush and in the celestial spheres, in the intricate web of the spider, and in the unfathomable soul of the human being.

For the rabbinic model of faith, a walk to work can be as profound an experience of faith as communal worship. It all depends upon the awareness and intention of the individual. The world's Divine foundation lays before us, awaiting discovery. So perfectly blended into the fabric of the world is God's presence that we are apt to miss it. But once noticed, it is like a trick picture in which we have suddenly seen the inner pattern. Like all true shifts in perception, we wonder how it ever went overlooked. But though God can be found, God cannot be proved. God cannot be intellectually demonstrated. There are arguments for and against the existence of God, as there have always been, but they are generally not what convinces or dissuades. God enters peoples lives not by proof but by presence. Reasoning is critical; as a rational faith, Judaism certainly does not wish to exile intellect. But just as description or logical deduction about another person is far less helpful in understanding him than a few minutes in his presence, an attempt to reach God abstractly through intellect does not stamp the soul as does reaching for a relationship with God.

Developing a relationship is not a logical, orderly process. Finding one's way to God can have all the wild, unpredictable exultation and disappointment of any other relationship but magnified, because this is one connection on which one must stake a soul. A tepid, polite relationship with God is nothing.

To draw close to God, according to the Rabbis, means to change one's life. Parts of ourselves will flourish, and other parts be put away. Our attitudes toward life and toward death are profoundly altered. Suddenly the universe is purposeful, where before it had been vain and empty. Suddenly our actions are of lasting import, our cries heard, our laughter and love not evanescent but part of the permanent pattern whose presiding Artist is close to us, near to our hearts. To have a relationship with God is to apprehend the world anew as a work of art whose outline is given but whose design and detail is our responsibility.

The God of the Rabbis is a God who searches for human beings as they search for God. The search takes place not only in history but in the daily doings of those whose passion permits them to see beyond the visible into the web of divinity that ties creation together. Each willing heart is God's dwelling place; the seeking itself is the first testimony of love.

A God of Passion

Judaism is not a cold faith, and its God is not a cold God. Some philosophers envision a God who is passionless, beyond all human categories and imaginings; but the God of the Jews is a passionate God, who not only created human beings but cares desperately about our choices and our fate.

In the Bible, God complains about the unfaithfulness of the people and about their evil deeds. Equally, God speaks about devotion to Israel, concern for humanity, love for the creations of this world. Like a passionate parent, an ardent mentor, and a hopeful friend, God in the Bible encourages and endures, seeking always to move humanity further along its journey.

In the Midrash, the collections of rabbinic legends, the Rabbis picture God in very emotional terms. God pleads, rages, even cries. These stories reflect the tremendous closeness the believer feels; the God of the Jewish tradition is not experienced as remote and removed. Rather, as the theologian Abraham J. Heschel has written, the God of the prophets and of later Jewish tradition is a God of pathos, a God of deep emotion.

In the Middle Ages, the Jewish poet and philosopher Yehuda Halevy drew a distinction between the "God of the philosophers" and the "God of Abraham, Isaac, and Jacob." The God of the philosophers is a God distant and unfathomable. The God of the patriarchs is a God of closeness, intimately bound up in human life and destiny. We may say that one idea of God is suitable for the classroom and the halls of academe, whereas the other walks with us through our days and nights, shares our sufferings, buoys our spirits, looks kindly on our triumphs and joys. Such a God is the God of legends, stories, of desert wanderings, and night-imaginings. Such a God may not fit the rigors of the philosopher, but such a God can be *felt*, and even in definitions we should not always give the head a veto over the heart.

Speaking to God

With God, we do not cry out to an empty universe. At times of sorrow and in times of joy, God's presence envelopes the believer in a conviction that passes all reason, the conviction that he or she is not alone.

It is to this presence that we pray. Prayer is a paradoxical activity; it involves passionate speaking to something one cannot see. That is one reason why during the most intense prayers worshipers will often close their eyes. We can be deceived by what we see, for the faculty of sight is so powerful, so overwhelming and immediate. But faith is triggered not in the senses but in the soul. That is why the Talmud teaches, "In prayer, one's eyes should be directed toward Jerusalem, and one's heart toward heaven."

The deepest prayer comes from need—but not from a need for wealth or healing or success. Rather, the deepest prayer comes from a need to pray. We speak to God to communicate with what is, to align our souls with the wonder that exists all around us. If we could picture prayer, it might look like we are scooping up inside our souls all the sparks of the Divine that we can reach and flinging them upward toward the heavens. The effort is great. True prayer is not an easy task. But equally great is the light that comes from us.

One's prayer is not heard, say the Rabbis of the Talmud, unless one places one's heart in one's hands. Real prayer happens when there is risk and hope and heart.

To be a Jew means to enter into a long-standing relationship. Much has passed between the Jews and God over the course of centuries. Any Jew who prays draws upon what has been said in the past, just as any speaker of language draws upon the images, ideas, expressions, and words of the generations who have gone before. No one invents a new language each time he speaks, and no Jew need begin to pray from scratch. There is a reservoir of prayers, petitions, and ideas from which to draw in our conversation with God. Yet in Judaism the past is not the totality of one's expression to God but only the beginning. Each worshiper forges his or her own path. Like a friendship, the Jewish conversation with God picks up each time against the background of the past and adds something new.

Speaking to God transcends words. There are rituals and actions that speak in ways more complex and deeper than any words. Lighting a candle, wrapping oneself in a tallit (prayer shawl), smelling the spices of the havadalah ceremony, placing mezuzahs on the portals of one's home—all these actions speak to God, touching and expressing the soul of the doer. To be Jewish is to inherit an extraordinarily beautiful language, a language invested with the genius and the dreams of millions of seekers.

Listening to God

To draw God into one's life involves not only speaking but listening. The Hasidic leader the Maggid (Preacher) of Mezeritch counsels that we "must be nothing but an ear which hears what the universe of the word is constantly saying within you. The moment you start hearing what you yourself are saying, you must stop." We must be able to silence ourselves for a while, to close off the sound of our own egos and hear a different kind of voice.

"The universe of the word" seems a strange and unexplainable phrase. Perhaps the Maggid is trying to tell us that there is a kind of speech, not exactly the way human beings speak to one another but one that still conveys both feeling and message. It is a speech that requires stillness and focus to hear. But all too often, we expect God to speak thunderously, in miracles and distinct revelations; lacking such "special effects," we decide that God must not exist.

In the Book of Kings, the prophet Elijah finds himself on a mountain. There, he experiences wind, earthquake, and fire, but the Bible insists that God is *not* in any of these powerful phenomena. Then comes a "still small voice," which, literally translated, is "the thin voice of silence." God is found in that voice (1 Kings 19).

Elijah learns the lesson of stillness. God does not grab us by the shoulders and shake us. God waits for the "drawing in," for the moments when we are able to take in the muted, even silent voice whose origin we recognize as being somehow beyond us. The Talmud speaks of the Rabbis of old preparing for hours before they began to pray. Speaking from the center of the soul takes preparation, and so does listening. We are instruments that must be tuned not only to produce music but to hear it.

Judaism is a lifelong training course in how to hear the sound of God in the world and in one's life. Along the way skills in speaking as well as in listening are learned, and a counterpoint emerges. Perhaps, as Heschel once wrote, God speaks slowly in our lives, a syllable at a time, and it is not until we reach the end of life that we can read the sentence backward.

Hearing and producing the music of faith takes time, but gradually, moments of transcendence become part of our lives. Then, like Elijah on the mountain, the earthquake seems small and insignificant next to the silent voice that thunders inside us.

Moments of Transcendence

There are moments that are granted, and moments that are created. At times, an overwhelming rush of experience will unlock a door to God. The birth of a child, a vision of beauty, perhaps a time of near catastrophe or genuine tragedy—when life hits extremes we are sometimes jarred into opening ourselves to the ultimate.

But it is a poor and untended faith—and an undisciplined soul—that reaches to God only in times of delight or distress. God in the Jewish tradition walks with us through each day, mundane as well as memorable, a companion not only of our emotional extremes but of the steady, small dramas of everyday life.

A life of spirit cannot be lived in special moments alone. Judaism cannot survive as a jewel in a glass case, to be taken out and displayed during holidays and life crises. Judaism seeks to teach us how to bring God into our lives, and our lives are made up of innumerable little stories, memories, fragments of thoughts and imaginings—the stuff of shopping and picnics and work and TV watching. Judaism insists that these moments, the ones we create, can be just as significant as the moments granted. God need not be absent from those activities. Each moment can open into transcendence. The gates of heaven are never bolted.

✦ ✦ ✦

Jewish ritual is *the discipline of pause and focus.* Perhaps the premier Jewish ritual, the Sabbath, forces one to pause, put down the distractions of life, and pay attention anew to the sounds of the soul and to God's place in our lives.

The Sabbath is often called a day of rest, but it is

equally a day of refocus. During the week we hear the sounds of the world changing and moving. The predominant rule of the Sabbath is to live in harmony with what is, not to seek change; this day is for renewal, not transformation. The Sabbath asks us not to be creative but restorative; not to give out but to take in; to sanctify time and recall our souls to their Source.

That is why so many of the seemingly restrictive rules of the Sabbath, such as a prohibition on spending money, are truly liberating. There is an Eastern poem that speaks about a violin string. Lying untouched on a table, the poet writes, the string is free. But it is not free to do what a violin string is supposed to do: to produce music. Only when it is strung and taut on the bow can it truly be free to be a violin string and offer its beautiful sounds. Discipline is critical for freedom. At certain times, ritual pares our lives to the core, so that we can hear and produce our true music.

◆   ◆   ◆

All rituals share in this essential feature of refocusing our attention. Before eating, reciting a blessing forces us to pause for a moment over the miracle of food and our relationship to God, from whom it sprung.

To pause is difficult because of the onrush of life.

There are places to go and tasks to perform. In our homes and cars, the voices on television or radio distract us. Reciting a blessing compels us to stop.

There is no tangible benefit to blessing food. With our practical orientation, we would not hesitate to pause if it would make the food taste better, but it seems so unproductive to pause to no "end."

But that is not the reasoning of relationship. It is a sound maxim of the marketplace not to waste time, but spirit grows in increments that cannot always be seen or felt. To grow toward God does not promise "practical" benefits: it will not enlarge bank balances or enhance careers; it deepens life and burnishes souls.

To bless bread does not make the bread taste better. The blessing deepens our appreciation for food and our connection to the Source of all sustenance.

Halakhah is the Hebrew word for Jewish law, and it literally means walking, a path to take and not a destination to reach. Jewish law is about reaching toward the center of one's soul, toward others, and toward God. The word *halakhah* reminds us that life is about the journey, not the arrival.

Traveling along that road both takes and teaches love of self and love of God. That love does not always arise naturally from the heart. Rather it comes from a life trained by and reflected in what Jewish ritual teaches us: both discipline and passion.

What Does God Want of Us?

Judaism is a vast system that seeks to spell out what it is that God wants from human beings. To summarize it in a few sentences is to simplify a complex and profound tradition. Nonetheless, we can perhaps draw two broad strokes to explain Judaism's approach.

Many Eastern religions speak of "mindfulness"— being in the present moment, aware and devoted to "the now." In the Jewish tradition, what God asks is *moral mindfulness*—to be always aware of the moral dimensions of our actions. Nothing exists in a vacuum; one is always in relation to others, always in the moral moment.

Moral mindfulness is the first thing that must govern our relationship to others. Ultimately there must also be *spiritual mindfulness*—an awareness of the presence of God behind all being and things in the world.

God is often sensed in sunsets and mountain ranges. Spiritual mindfulness asks us to see God all the time, to see the miraculous in the mundane. To reach these states of mindfulness requires commitment and discipline. But these two states, moral and spiritual mindfulness, should guide us in our relationship with others and with God.

By maintaining these awarenesses, we participate in the partnership that encourages *tikkun olam*, the repair of the world. By the disciplines of awareness, by observing the laws and practices that govern our conduct in this world, we are keeping up our part of the *brit*, the covenant of partnership. To do that requires commitment, awareness, discipline, and love.

✦ ✦ ✦

In raising children or training students, we understand that to enforce discipline with a wise, firm, but tender hand is to show love. Too often we forget that lesson when we ourselves are the students as well as the teacher.

A life of discipline shows esteem for one's own soul. If we truly treasure ourselves, we cannot permit ourselves to do just anything. Judaism maintains that God wants us to care enough for the inestimable gift we have been given, the gift of a unique soul, that we will show it the love of self-discipline. "He who has regard for his soul has regard for the commandments" (Prov. 19:16). The Bible is admonishing us that self-indulgence only *looks* like self-love. It is in *halakhah*, disciplined and deep journeying, that self-love is really found.

We can do God no real favors nor render God real services. Rather it is part of God's goodness that in serving God we are really enriching and deepening our own souls. The Jewish tradition insists that God not only created human beings but gave them the tools and wisdom to raise themselves above the physical dailiness of life into the realm of spirit. Moreover, Judaism teaches that to do so is our ultimate good. To glorify God is not for God's sake but for our own. To praise God's goodness is not to please or placate God but to remind ourselves of our own position and promise in this world. To humble ourselves before the Creator of the universe does nothing for the Creator of the universe; it does everything for the soul of the worshiper.

What God wants from us is that we should rise to the potential of the Divine spark within, not for God's sake but for our sake. We do it by a spiritual and moral mindfulness that arises from a life of disciplined love.

What Do I Want of God?

Many prayers thank God for the bounties of the world. We express our gratitude for the marvel of what is, for the marvel that *anything* is—that we have souls and a world to inhabit and enjoy. But of course we never seem to have quite enough, not for ourselves nor for others who may be in distress. So not only do we thank, we ask.

A great religious crisis waits in the asking, for we discover as children that to ask is not necessarily to receive. Somehow God's calculus of giving is very different from our own, and even when we see clear cases of pain and need, we cannot count on a hand dipping benevolently from the sky to bear up those who have fallen, to feed those who are hungry, to succor the many who feel bereft and alone.

Much of the time what we want of God is simple: that God should right the wrongs of this earth. Yet generation after generation, this longed-for end is denied.

◆　◆　◆

Perhaps what God seeks is not request but relationship, and we must learn to redirect our hearts to seek out not the goods that God could offer but to seek God.

◆　◆　◆

Many thinkers have tried to account for the existence of evil in God's world, and many different answers have been given.* But whatever the answer, one thing is clear: the moral order in this world requires struggle, and God will not make everything right in

---

*The interested reader can find a good survey in Louis Jacob's *A Jewish Theology* (New York: Behrman House, 1973). The reader interested in my own thoughts can find sections on the question in my previous books, most recently in *Teaching Your Children About God,* the chapter entitled "Why Does God Permit Evil?" (New York: HarperCollins, 1993).

response to an appeal, however heartbreaking and urgent.

So if God is not ultimately a gift store, if what we can get from God is not goods—neither material riches nor perfect health—what could we possibly want from God?

Here again we return to relationship. We have relationships with human beings even when they cannot render us services. What do we get from such relationships? Love, closeness, an ineffable filling up that surpasses description. Such rewards can be multiplied in a relationship with God.

What is it to have a relationship with something one cannot see? A relationship with God is a risk. It requires opening one's soul to the possibility that there will be only silence, emptiness, that the cosmos has nothing to offer other than the barrenness of space. That risk, more than all the intellectual objections and theological reservations in the world, keeps most people from faith.

But having taken that risk, the reward is unique. To feel a link with the Steward of the universe is to see the world and oneself in a different way. Creation is no longer indifferent; the space no longer seems vacant, an echoing emptiness. There is a God and an ultimate purpose.

Knowing that sufferings are heard and joy shared does not make everything perfect. Judaism is far too realistic a faith to maintain that any belief or connection can make life perfect. The best we are offered in this life is not paradise but partnership.

If we seek a never-failing recourse, our relationship with God is doomed to failure and disappointment. God will not always provide if provide means supplying the goods we need or want in this life. Many whose faith has rested on receiving have walked away from God empty-handed.

But if what we want from God is a sense that this world is not randomly spinning toward chaos, that we can feel close to the Author of all, that we can be filled with longing and love for our Creator, and that such a relationship can give us strength and purpose and courage, then we shall find God *does* provide these things. If we replace request with relationship and acquisitiveness with awe, we shall find that the God of Abraham and Sarah, of Isaac and Rebekah, of Jacob and Rachel and Leah, can have an intimate tie to us and to our lives as well.

There is a blessing in the Talmud that reads, "Blessed be God who knows secrets." A God who knows our secrets, who sees inside us, with whom we can share our innermost yearnings and fears—*and who loves us*—such a God gives us far more than those who have not sought God might ever imagine.

The Eternal One

"Oh God, you know the nature of man, for he is but flesh and blood. Man's origin is dust and he returns to dust . . . like a fragile potsherd, as the grass that withers, as the flower that fades, as a fleeting shadow, as a passing cloud, as the wind that blows, as the floating dust, as the dream that vanishes."

This declaration, from a prayer recited on Yom Kippur, the Day of Atonement, reminds us of our mortality. Each human life is a brief animate flourish before the darkness. We have but begun to live, and we are gone.

Perhaps because of the insecurity of life and the terror of its end, we strut our way in the world as though we were immortal and the cosmos cared for our good opinion. We do not admit to our own fragility, and our fear chokes off humility.

But that humility returns when we bring ourselves to confront God. Judaism speaks about *Yirat Hashem,* the awe one should feel before God. It is not a trembling fear but something greater. It is the sort of dumbstruck wonder one would feel before something astonishing, mighty, and otherworldly. If suddenly a mysterious force appeared before us, we would feel something of fear, of course, but our greater reaction would be sheer awe at the existence of such a thing in this world. As God is infinitely greater than the most awesome creation of our imaginations, our wonder should be beyond anything in our experience.

Such an attitude is threatening to human egos. We think well of ourselves, our talents and achievements. To bow before God seems unworthy, as though we were conceding part of our dignity. But a relationship to God is not a contest, and our self-esteem is not the winner's prize. Closeness to God is an enveloping embrace in the Eternal. If a life of spirit requires that we be in some way broken—as it does—it is not because God requires that we be humbled but because *we* require it, for no human being can be complete and full who does not know what it is to be broken and empty.

Humility is not a fashionable virtue in an age of assertiveness. But the humility we speak of does not mean that one cannot speak up at a job interview or a political rally. It is a deeper humility, a spiritual modesty that knows that human life is a flash, that most of our abilities are gifts, that life truly lived calls forth all of our energies and even more. It is the humility not of one who thinks himself worthless, but of one in awe of the soul he was granted, for it is in the image of God.

◆　◆　◆

Through ritual practices, community, prayer, history, and study, Judaism brings us closer to God. In the

Bible (Exod. 34) we are told that at times Moses wore a veil when appearing before the people, which he would remove when talking to God. As we draw close to God, we can remove our own veils—the masks that keep us partially hidden, that we wear for fear of being exposed, embarrassed, open before other human beings. Before God no one need hide or dissemble. There is expectation, to be sure, but also understanding. There is law but suffused always with love. God is the totality toward which our souls yearn.

CONCLUSION
Our Ultimate Fate

And should my spirit pass away,
God is with me—I will not fear.
Adon Olam

A prominent Jewish thinker, Leo Baeck, once
called Judaism a religion of "ethical optimism."
Judaism believes ultimately in the ability of human
beings to rise above their baser impulses and to improve this world. But along the way are tremendous
difficulties. So as with all faiths, Judaism must answer the question of whether it is *basically* optimistic.
Does Judaism believe, given all the suffering and sorrow of life, that this world is good?

The Jewish answer is a hesitant yes. The Jewish
people have suffered terribly, and over the centuries,
Jews have witnessed the horrible afflictions of so
many other nations and individuals. In the face of

that pain, to unthinkingly affirm how good the world is would be foolish and callous.

Yet this is also the world in which human beings have achieved nobly, created, loved, left enduring legacies for those who came after. In this world we have approached the idea of God and groped toward the reality that we are all part of the same family.

Surveying all the pain in this world, Judaism still insists that ultimately it is a good place. That faith is fundamental. The novelist Joseph Conrad certainly understood the evil and pain that exists in this world. Yet he wrote, "Woe to the man whose heart has not learned while young to hope, to love, and to put his trust in life." We hope for this world to be better, far better than it is today.

The optimism of Judaism has long taken the form of the concept of a Messiah, which some take to be an individual and others, symbolic of a messianic age. The messianic age will be a time when humanity will learn to put aside its viciousness and hate, and we will fulfill the Divine potential inside of us. In embracing the idea of messianism, Judaism has affirmed that history, despite its countless torments, will end in the triumph of goodness.

Belief in eventual redemption saves Judaism from the despair that plagues some faiths and the escape from reality that is the trademark of others. This world is not an illusion; it is a task. History is not an aimless chronicle of misadventures and brief brightnesses but a disorderly, effortful, and often pitiful march to something better.

In the meantime, lacking a Messiah, the most we can do is work to be worthy of such a time and seek to usher it in by virtue of our own effort and devotion.

This unredeemed world is plagued by evil of every description. Yet the imperfections of the world can lead us to overlook its splendor. Every feeling woman and man in this world knows it is far from ideal. But this world, in which we spend the brief decades that span human life, is good.

Yet it is not all.

Faith in the goodness of life and in the importance of the individual is what makes death so painful. If life is good, then death is tragic. Death may at times be welcome, but only when one has lost health or friends, when life has already sapped vigor and dreams.

Inevitably then, we wonder about our ultimate fate: what becomes of us after we die?

Judaism concentrates its energies and efforts on improving this world. As a result, it is often thought of as a this-worldly faith. The Torah, which is the foundation document of Judaism, says little about what happens to us after we die. Perhaps the Bible is deliberately silent, fearing that those who are always thinking of "another world" are of little help in this one.

Yet focusing on the world around us does not mean that we should never lift our eyes above the horizon. While Judaism does care most about the here and now, like all thoughtful traditions, there is speculation about what becomes of us after we die.

Judaism affirms that this world is not all, yet we cannot truly know what awaits us. Judaism urges humility before the mysteries of being. When even our greatest artists and thinkers conjure up other worlds, they are always composed of bits of this world—light, colors, natural beauty—all things we already know. It is simply beyond us to envision a different world, just as it would have been beyond us to envision this one before birth.

If we are sparks of the Divine, something in us is eternal. The particulars of that assurance are beyond our understanding. But it is the assurance and not the details that counts. Because our souls are linked to God, something of us will endure.

Judaism does insist on one thing: what one makes of one's soul here has something to do with what becomes of it later. That is why the Rabbis took such care to write two thousand years ago, "the righteous of *all* nations have a share in the world to come" (emphasis added). The corridors of eternity, however they wind, are open to all who live in a way that honors the spark of God inside them.

Judaism honors goodness wherever it is found and believes that God holds goodness and growth of spirit above any specific belief or allegiance. We cannot know precisely what the world to come will look like, but we can have a pretty good idea of the sorts of people Judaism teaches will live there in peace.

Traditionally, Judaism spoke of a Garden of Eden and Gehinnom, what we might call in modern English "heaven and hell." One represented a blissful afterlife; the other, retribution for terrible deeds on earth. The Garden of Eden comes from the biblical tale of Adam and Eve. Gehinnom is an actual place, a valley outside the walls of Jerusalem that one can visit to this day. Gehinnom was the site of pagan cults in the early days of Israel. Some of their members sacrificed children to appease and please their gods. To the Jews of antiquity, this practice was so awful that *Gehinnom* came to be the Jewish word for hell.

Some Jews have taken this idea literally, others see it as a metaphor—that souls condition themselves by their action, some producing an Eden, others a Gehinnom. Whatever the literal truth of the image, we can gain an important insight into the Jewish idea and ideals of eternity from the fol-

lowing: in 586 B.C.E., the Temple in Jeru
destroyed by the Babylonians. The Jews wɛɪɛ
iled from Jerusalem. It was the greatest calamity in
Jewish history until modern times. Even today,
Jews commemorate the catastrophe that befell them
when the Temple was destroyed.

A few years ago Israeli archaeologists came across
an amazing discovery. Just outside the walls of Jerusalem, the archaeologists found the burial cave of a
Jewish family. We know that this family had survived
the destruction because the artifacts in the cave were
dated from fifteen years after the Temple had been
burned to the ground. Perhaps even more remarkable, their tomb had not been pillaged by grave rob-
bers in the intervening centuries.

The grave was in the valley of Hinnom—Gehinnom
—the valley that became for Jews the symbol of hell.

When they cleared away the debris, the archaeologists found, among the pieces of pottery and
household objects, two amulets in the form of tiny
silver scrolls, just a few inches long. Crusted with
dirt and corrosion, they had been rolled shut for
2,600 years.

Working with painstaking care, opening them
gently and slowly, they found a barely legible inscrip-
tion, the oldest written section of the Torah we have.
Theretofore the oldest manuscripts had been the Dead

Sea Scrolls. These fragments predate the Dead Sea Scrolls by about seven hundred years.

The tiny amulets read, "May God bless you and keep you. May God cause his countenance to shine upon you and be gracious unto you. May God turn his countenance upon you and grant you peace."

A blessing for peace had been snatched from destruction, from the midst of hell on earth.

✦ ✦ ✦

Although we hope for a life after this one, our true task is to draw the powers of goodness into this world while we are here. There is much to do to turn this earth into an Eden, and we can only live in one world at a time.

✦ ✦ ✦

Why should one be Jewish? Because Judaism can teach us how to deepen our lives, to improve the world, to join with others who have the same lofty aims. Judaism can teach us spiritual and moral mindfulness, a way of living in this world that promotes joy inside of us and also encourages ethical action. But finally, the answer to why be Jewish must reside in the mystery of each seeking soul, trying to find its place with others and with God.

Growing in soul, seeking God, and helping the

world flourish are intertwined. Each moment of our lives is an opportunity to accomplish that task or to impede it. One reason to be Jewish is that Judaism gives us the inspiration, energy, and will to ensure that even from the midst of the valley of Hinnom a promise of Eden survives.

 . . . . Once a man or woman selects the city, he gives it his loyalty, his energy, and will to endure that

"GO AND LEARN"
For Further Reading

———————

One of the most famous stories in the Talmud involves a man who goes to see the great Rabbi Shammai. Tauntingly, he asks the Rabbi to explain Judaism while standing on one foot. Infuriated, the Rabbi drives the man from his house. The man then goes to another Rabbi, Hillel. In response to the same request, Hillel tells him, "What is hateful to you, do not do to another. That is the essence of the Law and the prophets. Now, go and learn."

Hillel's message is clear: how we behave in this world is the most important lesson of Judaism, but knowing that is only the beginning.

There are now more books published on Judaism in English than in any language at any time in history. Out of the many possibilities, I have included in this list some basic introductions to Judaism. Many of the books below have detailed bibliographies. Those with special interests—in Jewish mysticism, law, Bible, history, and so forth—should consult the bibliographies.

Ariel, David. *What Do Jews Believe?* (New York: Schocken, 1995).

De Lange, Nicholas. *Judaism* (New York: Oxford University Press, 1986).

Fishbane, Michael. *Judaism* (San Francisco: Harper and Row, 1987).

Gordis, Daniel. *God Was Not in the Fire* (New York: Scribner's, 1995).

Neusner, Jacob. *The Way of Torah* (Encino, Calif.: Dickenson Publishing, 1974).

Prager, Dennis, and Joseph Telushkin. *Nine Questions People Ask About Judaism* (New York: Simon and Schuster, 1981).

Steinberg, Milton. *Basic Judaism* (New York: Harcourt Brace, 1947).

———. *As a Driven Leaf* (New York: Behrman House, 1939). This is a novel brilliantly illuminating the world of the Rabbis.

Telushkin, Joseph. *Jewish Literacy* and *Jewish Wisdom* (New York: Warner Books, 1991, 1994).

Wouk, Herman. *This Is My God* (New York: Doubleday, 1959).

An exceptional book introducing the reader to the guiding ideas of the Sabbath and many of the most important ideas of Judaism is Abraham Joshua Heschel's *The Sabbath* (New York: Farrar, Straus and Young, 1951).

Two books that are guides to the Jewish book world are *The Schocken Guide to Jewish Books,* edited by Barry W. Holtz (New York: Schocken, 1992), and *The Book of Jewish Books* by Ruth S. Frank and William Wollheim (New York: Harper & Row, 1986). Some of my own favorites are listed in the annotated bibliography in the back of *The Healer of Shattered Hearts* (New York: Penguin, 1991).

Books can serve as guides, but they cannot replace community. There are synagogues in towns of almost any size as well as Jewish studies programs at local colleges and universities. Local synagogues and Rabbis are a marvelous place to start your journey. A trip to Israel can be the catalyst for a discovery of the meaning of the Jewish past and prospects for the Jewish future.

Each soul is unique, each journey individual, and each destination differently envisioned. But for all with the courage to explore, God awaits.

INDEX

About the Author

Rabbi David J. Wolpe is the author of three highly regarded books: *The Healer of Shattered Hearts: A Jewish View of God, In Speech and In Silence: The Jewish Quest for God,* and *Teaching Your Children About God: A Modern Jewish Approach.* Rabbi Wolpe has taught at the University of Judaism in Los Angeles and is presently Assistant to the Chancellor of the Jewish Theological Seminary in New York City. He lectures widely in the United States and abroad, speaking on Judaism and contemporary spirituality, and his columns are regular features in Jewish periodicals throughout the country.